The First Book of

*Creative Writing*

# The First Book of
# Creative Writing

by Julia C. Mahon

Illustrated by Gustave E. Nebel

Franklin Watts, Inc.
575 Lexington Avenue
New York, N.Y. 10022

The author's thanks to J. William Saunders, chairman of the English Department at Tourtellotte Memorial High School in North Grosvenor Dale, Connecticut, for his helpful suggestions regarding the manuscript of this book.

# Contents

The First Book of

Creative Writing

# 1. What Is Creative Writing?

From the dawn of history, man has felt a strong urge to express the things he has thought about or seen in the world around him.

The cavemen were hunters. Their lives depended on the bison, mammoths, deer, and tigers that they could kill for food. The hunt was vitally important to them.

Some of the cave dwellers, using charcoal, coloring material, and bone or wooden tools, drew on their cave walls outlines of the animals they hunted. But some could not be satisfied with these simple, isolated figures. They had to express the excitement of the chase, the tenseness of the fight, and the thrill of victory in bringing home the game.

So they began to draw picture stories on the walls. The first

1

group of sketches might have shown the cave women in their ceremonial hunt dance. Then came figures of many men leaving for the hunt. The next grouping showed these same figures, some in trees, some on the ground, at the moment when the game was sighted. Then the figures surrounded the animal with uplifted weapons; the animal was forced to the ground. Last of all came the triumphant return, with the game borne home by the hunters.[*]

Although primitive people may have drawn their picture stories for many practical reasons, such as religious fears and superstitions,

---

[*] Description based on picture story in Oscar Ogg's *The 26 Letters* (New York: Thomas Y. Crowell, 1961), pp. 24-25.

2

in one way they were the forerunners of creative writing. Without intending to, the cave dwellers showed in their art the most important elements of creative writing:

1. Plot. Simple though it was, the progress of the picture story showed a clear plot. It had purpose, conflict, and a solution of that conflict.
2. Characters. Here again was extreme simplicity, but the crude figures showed definite characters. The role of the women in their ceremonial dress was quite different from that of the hunters in the chase.
3. Style. This simply means a person's way of expressing his thoughts in writing. The more original the way, the more creative the writing. The picture stories on the cave walls were completely original.

Your dictionary gives several meanings for the word "create." One definition is "to produce from thought and imagination."*

If you think about this, you will soon have an excellent idea of what creative writing is.

---

* Funk and Wagnall's *Standard Dictionary*, International Ed., Vol. 1 (New York, 1960), p. 303.

# 2. Why Creative Writing?

What are your favorite indoor pastimes? Chances are that reading, television viewing, and movies rank high on the list.

Creative writing is the backbone of all of these, and many more. Every television program and every movie is based on a story written by someone somewhere.

And how about your schoolwork? Think of the subjects you enjoy most. Now think of your textbooks. Most likely, there is a strong connection between a favorite subject and an interesting textbook.

The books which give you the most knowledge and pleasure are those that present their subjects in a living, vital way. There is no dull recital of dry facts. Instead, it is as if a door were opened, showing you a new view of life. This ability to make you see clearly or feel deeply is the creative part of writing.

It is easy enough to see why we want and need creative writing. The question of why people write is not as easy to answer. In fact, it is very complicated.

You know the feeling you sometimes have in reading a good book — that you are in another world. You become so absorbed in the plot and the characters that you really seem to be there. It may surprise you to know that the author of the book felt much the same way.

No one knows exactly what makes a person become a writer. Perhaps it is partly a form of escape from the problems or pressures of everyday life. It may be the desire or the need to earn money. It may be the sheer joy of writing. Certainly there must be a need to communicate.

Perhaps you think you would like to become a professional writer. But whether or not you do, creative writing is important to you right now in school. So it is also important to find out what makes good writing good. Let us see how you can put more life into the forms of writing which are of most interest to you as a student.

# 3. Creativity in School Assignments

## The Composition

The composition, or essay, is a special joy to anyone interested in creative writing. It offers a wide freedom of choice. It may be short or long, funny or serious. It may poke fun at some accepted custom, or it may describe a beautiful nature scene.

A composition is not expected to treat its subject thoroughly. It may present any part of it, in any manner the writer chooses. But he must keep certain points in mind.

The first is that he must have something to say. This is where special interests come in. An important rule in writing is to stick to what you know. What kind of baseball story could you write if you had never seen a game? How well could you describe the beauty of the Irish countryside if you had never been to Ireland?

Perhaps you **will say**, "But what can I write about? I've never been anywhere or done anything."

The answer to that is another question: "You've lived, haven't you?" Anyone who has lived, anyone who has paid any attention at all to what goes on about him, has a thousand things to write about.

Think of your own home, wherever that may be. How about the excitement over your baby brother's or sister's first tooth? Or the night the lights went out? What about your mother's reaction when she found the new kittens in the closet?

9

What are your hobbies? Remember your first bicycle? What school activity is your favorite? Which do you like the least? Why? Your choice of subjects is practically endless.

Once the writer knows what he wants to say, his next job is to find an interesting way of saying it.

Let us suppose that you are one of the few people who dislike America's national sport — baseball. What happens if you begin your composition, or essay, with the bare statement, "I don't like baseball"? Most people would read no farther. They would simply dismiss the writer as a crank.

But suppose you begin another way: "This is a strange world we live in, where a man can get rich and famous by hitting a ball with a stick." The reader is apt to read on. Whether or not he agrees with your opinion, you will have made him see the matter in a little different light.

Style and the choice of words are important in holding the reader's interest. Don't be afraid to reread and rewrite your compositions. This polishing will result in better grades now and will be valuable practice for the writing you will do later on.

The following is an example of a humorous essay on a strange situation that occurred in everyday surroundings.

## Our Colorful Plumbing

One of the first things we discovered about our new home — which is an old house — was that we had highly original plumbing. Most pipes only carry water. Ours are different.

We found this out when Mother first washed vegetables in the kitchen sink. A short time later, Father called out loudly from the adjoining bathroom, "What the heck are carrot shavings doing in the bathtub?"

The following morning, there were coffee grounds in the bathroom washbasin. After lunch, there were broccoli buds in the tub.

Investigation proved that the pipes had not been laid at the right pitch for proper drainage. A plumber was called in. He spent a long time on his knees in the pantry, banging and sawing, and going out to his truck every now and then to get something else. When he finally finished, he scratched his head and said, "Well, that ought to help."

It did, in a way. When Mother washed vegetables the next day, more carrot curls than ever washed up in the bathtub.

Father said, "Well, I guess you can't have everything."

Mother said, "I knew we shouldn't have bought an old house."

Timmie, who has just learned to walk, held on to the side of the tub, peeking over, and laughed and laughed at the little curls of carrots.

I'm with Timmie. I am a little bit sorry for people whose pipes do nothing but carry water. Ours have imagination. They have variety. They have color. They have everything except proper pitch.

12

# The Book Report

Someone once said that nothing is certain in this world except death and taxes. As a student, you might add one more item: the book report. It is not hard to understand why teachers assign book reports. They encourage reading; they teach you to analyze, to develop a sense of critical judgment.

All good book reports should include the title, author, publisher, and date of publication. With these details out of the way, the following questions should be answered:

1. What do you think was the author's purpose in writing this book? Was he trying to entertain? Was he criticizing something?
2. How well did he succeed? Were you amused? Did it make you feel angry or sad?
3. Do you think the book was worth writing? Will many people enjoy it? Do you feel it may accomplish some good?
4. What is your opinion of the author's style? Is it smooth and easily read, or did you find it difficult to follow?

In reporting on fiction, you might comment on the plot. Did it hold your interest? How about the characters? Did they seem real? Did the story have some special setting which influenced it? A story set in the Civil War, for example, would be greatly influenced by this factor.

If you are reporting on biography, comment on the author's view of his subject. Did he try to make the person seem perfect? Or did he bring out human faults?

Don't be afraid to give your honest opinion. Just be sure that you can give your reasons for thinking as you do. This is what your teacher wants. It is what makes the book report *yours*. It will have the stamp of originality. And this is the most important element in any creative writing.

Here is an example of a book report:

Title:   *Where the Panther Screams*
Author:   William P. Robinson
Publisher:   World
Copyright date:   1961

How would you like to leave your home and your friends and move into a wild country? This is what happened to Joe Hawkins in *Where the Panther Screams.*

It is a story of the hardships faced by the pioneers who settled the Oklahoma Territory. Joe's pa is burning with eagerness to go west; his mamma wants to stay in their comfortable home. Mr. Hawkins wins, but wherever they go she clings stubbornly to her prized blue bowl. To her it represents the peaceful, orderly life they left, and her hope for the future.

The author has told an exciting story of life in the Old West. A tornado wipes out the beginning of the Hawkins family's new home, which had cost them weeks of hard work as well as money. Wolves and coyotes threaten their livestock. From time to time, the scream of the panther splits the air, freezing them in their tracks.

I like this story. It is well written; it has a lot of action; and the people in it act and talk like real people. The author shows how courage and determination can win out over the most difficult circumstances.

# The Short Story

A short story has several marks to identify it. It usually has only one or two main characters. The events in it are usually not drawn out over years, as they might be in a novel, but take place within a short span of time. The action is usually limited to a few incidents, and it produces a single impression. You remember a short story as being a funny story or a sad one or a scary one, but not all three at once. The writer cannot afford this; in a short story he must make every word count toward the idea and mood he is trying to put across to his reader.

The most important elements in a story are the people in it, the plot, the setting, and the writer's style. Short stories are usually told from the viewpoint of a third person, but sometimes the first-person form is used.

The third-person form means that the characters are referred to as *he* and *she*. The first-person form puts the writer directly into the story. It sounds as if he were talking to the reader.

The excerpt from *Little Women* on page 31, and the book report on *Where the Panther Screams* on page 16, are examples of third-person form. The composition, *Our Colorful Plumbing* on page 12, and the short story, *My Dad, the Outlaw* on page 19, are examples of how the first-person form is used.

The advantage of the third-person form is that it gives the writer more freedom of expression. Because he is not supposed to be present in the story — at least not obviously present — he can describe what happened in various places or different times.

The first-person form restricts the writer in this sense. The action, as a rule, is limited to what one person sees or hears. But there is also an advantage in this form. It has more personal appeal. If a person tells you how he feels about something, you find it much more convincing than if he tells you how somebody else feels about it.

This is an example of a short story told in the first person:

## My Dad, the Outlaw

My dad looks and sounds like a mild-mannered man. He carries an umbrella when it rains, and he would never sit when a lady was standing. Practically nobody would believe that for a little while he was a desperate criminal. But it's true. It happened like this:

Dad sells real estate. The day he and I were to drive into New York to meet my Aunt Clara, Dad said we'd have to go by Fairmont to a

house he had for sale. On the way, he told me about the lady he was to meet there.

She was a widow; she had looked at the house before but couldn't quite make up her mind about it. She had asked for the key so she could go in this afternoon and look at it again. My dad said sure, he would meet her there.

"Poor woman," he said. "She has several young children. When she told me they had to catch a train back to New York this afternoon, I invited them to drive in with us."

Fairmont is a nice little Connecticut town. The houses are neat and clean-looking. The house for sale is on Audubon Street. As we drove toward it, we could see the door was partly open.

"Good," said Dad. "She's there. I'd hate to be delayed and keep Clara waiting."

There was a cute little boy sitting on the steps. He had blue eyes and round, rosy cheeks, and a wisp of blond curl stuck out under his red knitted cap. He smiled at my father as we came up the steps, and held out his arms. I could see my father was pleased. He laughed and swung him up in his arms. The little boy held Dad tight around the neck, smiling.

At this moment, a blonde girl about four years old stuck her head out the door, then drew it back quickly.

"He's here, Mama! He's here! He's here!" we could hear her saying. A soft voice answered, "Sh-h-h . . . don't get so excited, Mary Lou."

We went in. Dad introduced me to Mrs. Coulter, then she introduced the others. Mary Lou we had seen. A blond, shy-looking boy of about ten was Luke; a slightly taller girl with brown curly hair was Janice. Dad greeted all of them in a nice, polite way; then he grinned broadly, looking down at the head of the little fellow who still held him tightly around the neck.

"And I call this fellow my buddy," Dad said.

"He looks like your buddy," Mrs. Coulter answered, with a smile. "Well, Mr. Dawson, I've decided definitely. The house is just what we want. The size is good, it's a nice neighborhood, and we'll be near my

21

sister. We might as well go on our way now. We can talk in the car."

They all filed out and Dad locked the door. Mrs. Coulter got in the backseat with her children, so I got in the front. Dad came down the walk, the little boy clinging happily to him.

"Everybody all set?" Dad asked. "Okay, Buddy, you go in with me!" He swung the little boy in over the steering wheel, then got in himself.

The little boy rested against Dad, his head against his shoulder. "Bye-bye," he was murmuring to himself, smiling.

"You can see he likes to ride," said my father.

"You certainly can," said Mrs. Coulter.

They started talking about the house, financial arrangements, and all that kind of stuff. It went on for a long time. Then they started about schools and bus transportation. I didn't want to be rude, but I sure wished we could hear something else. I asked Dad if I could put on the radio. He said yes, if I kept it quiet. I looked back at Luke and Janice. They both grinned. I could see I wasn't the only one who wanted to hear something else.

I turned the dial. A shrill, false-sounding voice was saying how much you could save at McDonald's store. A deep voice bellowed out some kind of music. An excited voice was saying something about a kidnapping. Suddenly I recognized the notes of a Beatle record. I looked sideways at Dad. He and Mrs. Coulter were absorbed in their conversation. I relaxed and settled back to hear the Beatles.

We were getting close to New York now. The buildings were zipping past the windows in an almost unbroken stream.

"Tell me where to turn off for your place," Dad said.

"I will," she answered. "It isn't very far."

The program was interrupted by news of a two-year-old child who had been kidnapped that afternoon.

"How awful," said Mrs. Coulter. "Can you imagine anyone cruel enough to do a thing like that?"

"No, I can't," said Dad. They went on talking, so I turned to another station and another record.

22

"The next turn left is ours," said Mrs. Coulter at last. They had agreed on financing, and she said she would be back in Fairmount the next weekend to sign the papers.

"The next street right is ours," she said. We turned in and stopped at the brownstone house she indicated. The Coulters got out of the backseat. Luke and Janice and Mary Lou said good-bye.

"I can't tell you how much I appreciate your bringing us home, Mr. Dawson," said Mrs. Coulter. Dad said she was quite welcome. He opened the front door and started to hand the little boy out to her. She just stared at him with a queer, puzzled look. She made no move to take the little boy. Dad sort of froze, with the strangest look on his face. They just kept staring at each other, then at the child.

"But isn't he yours?" my father asked at last.

"Why, no," she said. "Isn't he yours?"

I thought I knew my father pretty well, but I have never seen him look like that. "Put on the radio," he said. I turned it on.

"A massive manhunt is on for the kidnapper of Franklin Evans, Jr., of Fairmont, Connecticut," a voice was saying. "The two-year-old child was taken from his home on Audubon Street this afternoon. His mother said he had been in the yard for only a few minutes. A neighbor down the street said she saw a man put the child in his car and drive away. She described the man as being of medium height and wearing a gray overcoat. She said the car was dark blue. It was her impression that there was someone else in the car."

My father was gazing at the hood of our dark-blue car. He looked down at his gray overcoat. He sighed.

"Let's go," he said in a strangled voice.

That ride back was the longest I have ever had in my life. It must have been close to an hour before we even thought of Aunt Clara. Then all my father said, in that same queer tone, was, "Clara will have to wait."

There were several cars in front of the house next to Dad's on Audubon Street. One was a police car; one bore a doctor's symbol.

25

My father sighed deeply and reached over to pick up the little boy, who was sleeping peacefully against him. Dad sighed again. He started up the walk toward the house, with me a few feet behind him.

That's the time my dad was a desperate criminal. And if you could have seen his face as he walked into that house full of people, with the little boy in his arms, you would know exactly what I mean by desperate.

# 4. The Four Basic Elements in Writing

## Plotting

The plot is one of the most important elements in any fiction, and especially in the short story. A well-developed plot is one that seizes the reader's interest immediately and holds it to the very end.

Plotting has two chief aspects, conflict and progress. Most plots contain both.

Conflict means that the main character must have some obstacle to overcome. This may be a physical, or outside, obstacle, such as another person, an animal, or some natural danger that threatens him or prevents him from attaining a certain goal.

In the book *Where the Panther Screams*, the Hawkins family faces several kinds of obstacles: the tornado that destroys their house; the hardships; the wild animals that threaten the family and the livestock. In fact, from the very beginning, the opposing attitudes of Mr. and Mrs. Hawkins represent conflict. His desire to go west is an obstacle to her wish for a peaceful life; her wish for peace is an obstacle to his yearning for adventure.

In *Little Women*, by Louisa May Alcott, the poverty of the family is an obstacle to the girls' ambitions. Their father's absence in the war is an obstacle to their family unity. Obstacles posed by illness, worry, and tragedy are interspersed with warm, humorous episodes to keep the reader entertained and engrossed in what will follow.

A story must also have some type of progress. This may be actual, natural progress toward a set goal, as Mr. Hawkins' move west was. Or it may be an inner type of progress in which a character faces and overcomes an inward struggle. This would be the case with a hot-tempered character, for example, or one who strives to conquer a strong dislike for another.

Conflict and progress, used thoughtfully, result in a gripping plot.

Imagine that you want to write about a boy named Tim who enters a soapbox derby. If you simply tell how Tim makes a car from a wooden box, enters, and either wins or loses the race, you will not have much of a story.

But try putting in some conflict and an obstacle or two. First, give Tim an urgent reason for wanting to win. Then introduce another boy who also wants badly to win — who wants it so badly, in fact, that he plots against Tim, doing something to damage Tim's entry in the race.

Now really get into your story, building up the excitement and tension to the climax. You have a plot now that will keep your reader eager to see the ending, whatever it may be. Tim might win and teach the other boy that dishonesty does not pay. Or Tim might lose, but recognizing that the other boy had a more serious reason for needing to win, he might forgive him and thus teach the boy an unforgettable lesson in generosity.

A good method of plotting a short story is to make a statement at the beginning which is surprising enough to make the reader follow it to see how it will develop. This is what was done in the short story, *My Dad, the Outlaw*.

Whatever method is used, a good plot is a quality that will make the reader enjoy and remember a story.

## Bringing Characters to Life

The characters in a story are just black lines on white paper until the writer breathes life into them by making them seem real to his readers.

How can this be done? There are several ways. The writer may tell what the character is like. He may let someone else in the story describe him. Or he may let the character speak for himself.

The last way is the best. Good dialogue, or conversation, gets the reader involved in a story faster and more completely than any other single thing.

Let us look at the beginning of a story that has been read and loved by millions of people for nearly a century. The book is *Little Women*. It starts like this:

## Little Women

"Christmas won't be Christmas without any presents," grumbled Jo, lying on the rug.

"It's so dreadful to be poor!" sighed Meg, looking down at her old dress.

"I don't think it's fair for some girls to have plenty of pretty things, and other girls nothing at all," added little Amy, with an injured sniff.

"We've got father and mother and each other," said Beth contentedly, from her corner.

The four young faces on which the firelight shone brightened at her cheerful words, but darkened again as Jo said sadly:

"We haven't got father, and shall not have him for a long time." She didn't say "perhaps never," but each silently added it, thinking of father far away, where the fighting was.*

\* \* \*

Now go back to Jo's first words. What was your reaction to them? Very likely it was something like this: Christmas without any presents? How awful! But why?

---

\* Louisa May Alcott, *Little Women* (New York: Grosset & Dunlap, 1947), pp. 3-4.

See what a clever writer did with her very first sentence? She aroused your sympathy for the leading character. She captured your interest in what was to come. She also told you a good deal about Jo herself. Here was no martyr, suffering silently or cheerfully, but a human being who grumbled at disappointment.

Even her position revealed something about Jo. This book was written a hundred years ago when well-bred young ladies did not lie on rugs. Jo was a tomboy.

In the next few lines, Miss Alcott gave clues to what would soon be obvious about the other girls: Amy's vanity; Beth's gentle, peace-loving nature; and Meg's rather lofty opinion of herself as the oldest sister. The warm relationship between the girls was shown.

This is what good dialogue can do. It can draw the reader right into the story and keep him there.

What makes dialogue good? First, it must sound like people do sound when they are talking — easy and natural, not stiff and stilted.

Second, it must be consistent with the character being presented. If you intend to show Mary as a kind, generous person, you cannot have her speak kindly one moment and harshly the next. This would only confuse your readers and certainly would enlist no sympathy for Mary. Generally speaking, everything Mary says should add to the word picture of her. Then, if in a scene of extreme anger or grief, she does speak harshly, it will be very effective, showing just how far she was pushed. And, of course, it will show that she is human in spite of her virtues.

Describing the person you are writing about is a help toward bringing that character to life. People like to know how other people look, in real life or in fiction. You may do this directly or indirectly. You may tell about Ned's appearance yourself, or you may have another character in the story do it this way:

"Mary admired Ned. She thought him very handsome, with his clean-cut features, hazel eyes, and light-brown hair. She liked the erect way he stood and the easy, swinging grace with which he walked."

The most important thing in making characters seem real to others is to have them seem real to yourself before you start writing. Think about Ned and Mary: about what kind of people you want them to be. Let them grow and develop in your mind until you can feel their personalities. Then it will be easy to write about them. In fact, if they become real enough to you, you can practically let them take over the story!

## Setting

The setting of a story is the quality you might consider of the least value, but it has an importance all its own.

Think of the last story you read. What was its setting? You might be tempted to answer that it had no special setting. But think again. Suppose it was a school story. Now that you reflect on it, you realize that the reason you did not notice the setting much was that it was all so familiar to you: the squeak of the chalk on the blackboard, the shuffle of feet in the aisles, the surge of elation at the dismissal bell.

Could that story have been the same without this setting? Of course not. And the fact that it seemed so familiar to you is proof that it was done by a skillful writer.

In some stories, the setting is of such vital importance that it might be said to play the leading role. This would be true of a story set in a war, for example. Or one which took place on a raft or a lifeboat.

In any case, the effectiveness of your story will depend, to some extent, on how vividly you can make the reader "feel" the setting. Let us look at a few examples:

Charlie was at the seashore.

Charlie felt the warm sand grow cooler under his feet as he approached the water's edge. The white rim of a wave curled and rippled about his toes in little foaming bubbles.

In the second example, you not only know that Charlie is at the seashore, but suddenly you are there with him.

Or how about this:

Chris went into the kitchen.

Chris opened the kitchen door. After the biting chill of the cold outside, the warm, steaming fragrance of coffee and bacon was like a blessing.

Here again, you enter the kitchen with Chris. You know what it is to come in from the cold to the sweet warmth of home and food.

Why simply state that Mary went to milk the cow? Make your

34

reader feel the cool breeze against Mary's face, hear the plaintive lowing of the cow, smell the pungent odor of the barn.

When you put Ned in a ball game, let your reader hear the triumphant crack of the bat against the ball, and feel the pounding of Ned's heart as he races for the base.

These details give your setting life and color. They capture the interest of a reader just as convincing characters and a well-executed plot do. Each plays its own part to draw the reader into the story, to make him feel a part of it.

## What Is Style?

Style is the way a person expresses himself in writing. If he uses words with care, with simplicity and precision, his style will be one of charm and easy grace.

No teacher can give his students style. He can teach them rules of composition and grammar, but style is a quality that each must develop for himself.

It is something like speech put on paper. Think of the differences in the ways your friends talk. Jane is very quiet; she uses words sparingly. Fred talks fast and at great length; words literally pour from him. Bill tends to hesitate between sentences, as if searching for the exact phrase. Sue speaks crisply and with emphasis.

The style of different writers is like this. Notice how some write briefly, with short sentences, while others use long sentences and paragraphs.

The first step — and the last — toward achieving style is simply this: to write. Write about the things that interest you most, in the way that comes most naturally to you. Then look with a critical eye over what you have written and start correcting. Have you arranged your thoughts in an orderly way? Have you used the best words for what you wanted to say? Have you expressed your thoughts as clearly as possible?

Probably not. Few writers, even good ones, produce fine results on their first draft. The answer is to revise and rewrite as often as is necessary.

If a sentence seems too long to you on rereading, break it up and make two shorter, more concise sentences. Have you used an adjective that is not really needed? If so, take it out. Have you used a flat, colorless verb? Couldn't you think of a more vigorous one?

So you write and write and write some more. And all the time, strangely enough, it is becoming easier and easier to express yourself. Then one day your teacher, or someone else whom you respect and admire, will say something wonderful to you: "You know, you have a nice style."

# 5. The Importance of Grammar

When a person starts to build something, he is — or he ought to be — concerned about several things. He should know that his materials are good and that they will fit what he plans to construct. He needs to be sure that he has the right tools for the job. He must be able to use these tools.

Can you imagine a carpenter trying to get along with a screwdriver when he really needs a wrench? Or can you imagine his attempting carpentry at all if he had never seen a saw or a lathe?

The better the materials, the tools, and the skill of the builder, the better the construction will be. If any of these is faulty, the building will suffer.

So it is with writing, too. Ideas are the materials the writer begins with. Words are his tools. He must develop skill in using these.

The more a writer values his ideas, or believes in them, the more he should strive for excellence in expressing them.

You may have seen someone called on unexpectedly — perhaps on television — to give his opinion of some event. It is a sorry sight to see a person grope and stumble for words, and never really make much sense. The worst of it is that this person might have sound ideas, but his inability to express them makes them useless.

This is even more true of writers. It is very sad to hear someone say, "I love to write, but somehow I just can't put down on paper what I want to say. It never sounds right."

# 6. Choosing Words

## The Vital Verb

Of all the words you can use in creative writing, none is more versatile or more vital than the verb. The verb carries the action; it packs the punch.

If you doubt this, let us see for a moment what changing a verb can do to a mental picture. Pause for a few seconds after reading each of the following sentences. Let its impression sink in before you go on to the next.

"Will you go?" she whispered.
"Will you go!" he snarled.
"Will you go!" she screamed.

The weakest verb you can use in writing is the verb "to be" in any of its forms. It conveys no action at all; it simply states that a thing exists. There are many times when this verb should be used, but if you wish to give force and color to your writing you can use many other verbs that carry more punch. See the difference it can make:

Jim was in the ball game.
Jim pitched a two-hit shutout in the game.

In the second sentence, both Jim and the ball game come to life. That's what you want, isn't it?

A lot of leaves were lying on the ground.
Scarlet leaves carpeted the ground.

Which of the above sentences not only paints a mental picture but makes you feel the soft crunch of autumn leaves underfoot?

Try experimenting with verbs on your own, changing the drab and colorless to livelier ones:

The new girl seemed friendly but shy.
The new girl greeted us with a shy but friendly smile.

Lombardy poplars grew along the lane.
Rows of Lombardy poplars guarded the lane.

The right verb can convey the idea or mood you want to put across swiftly and neatly. Suppose you say:

Scott walked along the sidewalk to school.

What are you telling your reader about Scott? Practically nothing. Hundreds of children in that same town are doing the very same thing. But suppose you say:

Scott bounded along the sidewalk to school.

Your reader perks up. What is Scott so excited or eager about? What's going to happen?

Or suppose you say:

Scott trudged along the sidewalk to school.

There is the same sort of reaction from your reader. What's the matter? Why is Scott so reluctant to go to school? What's going to happen?

This last little question is most important to a writer. As long as he can keep his reader asking it, he can keep his reader. Verbs play a vital role in holding the reader's interest. They make the difference between lively, colorful writing that excites, and dull, plodding writing that bores.

Words are the writer's tools. There is not one tool more valuable than the verb. It is the hinge on which the whole sentence swings.

## The Necessary Noun and Proper Pronoun

If verbs are viewed as the muscles in writing, then nouns might be called the bones. The verbs pull and swing; the nouns are rigid, moving only as the verbs propel them. Yet the nouns are as necessary to the form of the sentence as the bones to the body.

While nouns in themselves are not flexible, as verbs are, there are ways of getting some variety in their use. A good method is to study a dictionary of synonyms; this suggests a number of words, including nouns, which may be used in place of other words.

Suppose you were writing a story about the President of the United States. It would get pretty monotonous if you had to use the noun "President" every sentence or so. But you could use his name, or call him the Chief Executive or Chief of State. Using synonyms avoids boredom.

Every writer who takes his work seriously should make use of a dictionary of synonyms from time to time.

The pronoun is a valuable little substitute for variety in writing. You would not want to keep repeating "Mary" or "Mary's" each time your heroine is mentioned, and certainly your reader would not want to keep reading the name, again and again. It is quick, convenient, and easy all around to be able to use "she" or "hers" instead of repeating the noun.

But this little tool can be dangerous if not properly used. Instead of keeping your reader from getting bored or irritated by repetition, which is its purpose, it can confuse him completely.

The chief law of pronouns is this: *Never use a pronoun without making certain that its reference is clear.*

Look what happens when this rule is forgotten:

Sue walked with Jane to the door. She gave her her coat.

Who gave a coat to whom? Was Sue merely doing what the hostess would be expected to do for a departing guest? Or was Jane, in a burst of generosity, making Sue a present of a coat? How could the reader know? See how this way of writing the sentence clarifies the matter:

As the two girls walked to the door, Sue handed Jane's coat to her.

Using exact quotes can also be a help in keeping pronouns in order.

How about this?

Dick told his brother he was getting a puppy for his birthday.

Can you tell which boy was getting the puppy? You can't, and neither can anyone else. Yet either of these statements makes it perfectly clear:

Dick said to his brother, "You are getting a puppy for your birthday."
Dick said to his brother, "I'm getting a puppy for my birthday."

*You* know what you mean when you write because the thought was first formed in your own mind. Your concern must be to make the reader know what you mean. It will not be in his mind, exactly as you planned it, until you put it there.

Many times a noun is called for instead of a pronoun to make the meaning clear:

Ned called Spot and put the rolled newspaper in his mouth.

How can you know what this sentence means? Was Ned showing how smart his dog was, or was Ned himself clowning with the newspaper in his mouth? A substituted noun clears up the confusion:

Ned called Spot and put the rolled newspaper in the dog's mouth.

48

Beware of the reference to a noun hidden in the possessive case! This is wrong:

Tom went to Chicago to his aunt's house, whom he had never seen.

This is right:

Tom went to Chicago to the home of his aunt, whom he had never seen.

Just as good bone structure is important to a healthy, active body, so the proper use of nouns and pronouns plays its part in vigorous creative writing.

# The Ask-Adjective

Adjectives are to writing what salt and pepper are to food. Used sparingly, they add seasoning to flavor. Sprinkled about too freely, they detract from the reader's enjoyment and can even spoil everything for him.

Many years ago, in the last century, it was the habit of inferior writers to pile one adjective on top of another. They seemed to think that this made their statements stronger. Actually, it did just the opposite.

Take a sentence like this:

The terrible fire was an awful, horrible tragedy.

Strip away the unnecessary adjectives and see how much more impact it carries:

The fire was a tragedy.

In planning a sentence, learn to ask one question: "Is this adjective necessary?" If you can answer no, the adjective should go.

This does not mean, of course, that adjectives should never be used. It means that they should be used carefully and thoughtfully. There are times when one, or even two, are needed to say exactly what you want to say.

Take the case of the poet who wrote of waves breaking on cold gray stones. Were these adjectives unnecessary? Of course not.

You suddenly see the leaden color of sea stones; you feel the wet chill of sea spray on barren rocks. The poet needed both of these for the word picture he wished to paint.

Generally speaking, however, you will make your own word pictures more vivid with detailed description than with a string of adjectives. Take this example:

The stranger was a big, burly, cruel-looking man.

The stranger towered over the other men. His shoulders were massive and his arms were knotted with muscles. He looked through narrowed eyes; his lips turned down at the corners in a sneer that seemed to be one of his features.

Which stranger would you remember?

Adjectives are perfectly respectable words and can be quite valuable to the writer. Just remember to ask yourself the question in using them — are they necessary? You want a delicate flavor in your writing, not a concoction in which too much seasoning has spoiled the taste.

# 7. How to Do Research

## Using the Library

The reports you are assigned in school demand a special kind of preparation. It is called research.

It seems unfortunate that such a technical-sounding word has to be used for something that can be so much fun. All research really means is finding out about something. And this can be a kind of treasure hunt, gathering the bits and pieces of information that you need to work into a good report.

There is a real treasure-house available to you for this purpose. It is your library.

The library contains a store of information on practically every subject. It is important to everyone, and especially to a student or a writer, to know how to use the library.

The card catalog is the key to the library, and if you have ever used a library you are familiar with this cabinet containing many small drawers with lettered labels. In each drawer are cards beginning with the letters that are listed on the front. These cards represent all of the books to be found in the library. They are filed in alphabetical order by title, author, and subject.

So if you were doing a book report on *Big Red*, but had forgotten the author's name, you would look in the B drawer. There under the title would be the name Jim Kjelgaard, the author of the book. This is called a title card.

Or if someone told you there were some exciting books by Robb White in the library, you would look in the W drawer for White, and there you would find the names of his books. The cards that list the author first are called author cards.

If you had to do a report on snakes and didn't know of any books on them, you would look in the S drawer. Under the word SNAKES, in capital or red letters, you would find a number of cards listing books on this subject. These are called subject cards.

The library has a great many other valuable aids to help you in your research. A major one is the encyclopedia. Encyclopedias have information on many persons, places, and things, arranged in alphabetical order from A through Z.

For short reports, you may find as much material as you need in one volume of the encyclopedia. For longer ones, you might consult the suggested outlines at the end of some articles. These can

be of much assistance in organizing your material. A list of related articles may also be given. If so, study this list and decide which of the topics listed will add interest and variety to your report.

Never copy the material in an encyclopedia. The person who wrote whatever article you choose used his own brain and talent to compose it. Use yours. To copy someone else's work is dishonest, and it is also an insult to your own intelligence and ability. Read the article, get the facts, then set them down in your own language, in your own style.

For articles on current events, go to the *Abridged Reader's Guide to Periodical Literature*. This will refer you to recent magazines for accounts or opinions on current affairs. Ask your librarian how to use it.

Other special helps for you in the library are the atlas, the globe, the unabridged dictionary, the almanac.

Learn all you possibly can about your library and the books in it. The library is truly a treasure-house, a place where you can greatly enrich your mind and your work.

## The Noteworthy Notebook

Although the library is your chief source of reference, it is certainly not the only one.

Suppose you wanted to write a report on model railroads and you heard that a man in your town made a hobby of model railroading. You might get enough information from him to make a fine report.

This is where an important part of creative writing comes in — taking notes. You should jot down notes as the man explains to you the operation and equipment of the model railroad. It would take much too long to write down everything he said, but if you didn't write down anything, you would forget much of it. You also might make mistakes later in writing down what you *did* remember. Good notes — a brief summary of the key points — are extremely helpful to a writer.

You should get in the habit of taking along a small notebook when you are looking for information on a subject, whether you are talking with someone informally or listening to a formal speech. A single word or phrase can bring back to mind a whole paragraph or more when you read it later.

But always remember that if you plan to quote a speaker, do not trust his words to memory. Take down his words exactly and do so at the time he says them. Anything appearing in quotation marks should be precisely, word for word, what the speaker actually said. Any other words would be both irritating and unfair to the speaker. It would also be unfair to anyone reading your report.

People have a right to expect that a writer knows what he or she is writing about. They have a right to believe that a person said what he is quoted as having said. To be inaccurate in reporting is sloppy work on the part of the writer.

Another situation in which a notebook will prove invaluable is a visit to a place you want to write about. Vivid bits of description jotted down while you are under the spell of a beautiful spot will add color and charm to the account you will write later. A detailed depiction of a historical place will provide an authentic setting for a story or article.

In fact, there are times when you may come to feel that your notebook is an integral part of your writing equipment. Well used, it can be a brimming source of the colorful details which are so much a part of creative writing.

❋   ❋   ❋

# Index